A POCKET GUIDE TO

Amish Life

MINDY STARNS CLARK

HARVEST HOUSE PUBLISHERS

EUGENE, OREGON

Cover photo © Diane Diederich

Cover by Dugan Design Group, Bloomington, Minnesota

Illustrations by Amy Hanson Starns.

Mindy Starns Clark is represented by MacGregor Literary.

A POCKET GUIDE TO AMISH LIFE
Copyright © 2010 by Mindy Starns Clark
Published by Harvest House Publishers
Eugene, Oregon 97402
www.harvesthousepublishers.com

ISBN 978-0-7369-2864-9

Printed in the United States of America

10 11 12 13 14 15 16 17 18 / BP-SK / 10 9 8 7 6 5 4 3 2 1

CONTENTS

Dedicated to the kind Amish folks who answered my questions, aided my research, and made me feel welcome. Your graciousness and transparency have been a tremendous blessing!

Acknowledgments

Many, many thanks to John Clark, my sweet husband and favorite research partner.

Thanks also to Emily and Lauren Clark, Amy Starns, Erik Wesner, Dave Siegrist, Gene Skinner, Chip MacGregor, ChiLibris, Shari Weber, Vanessa Hart, Dee Benjamin, Ned and Marie Scannell, Larry and Bebe Hebling, Kim Moore, and everyone at Harvest House Publishers. Thanks also to Steve and Jamie Shane of the Apple Bin Inn in Willow Street, Pennsylvania; the Mennonite Information Center in Lancaster, Pennsylvania; and all the members of my online advisory group, Consensus.

A portion of the proceeds from this book will be donated to Amish-related nonprofit organizations. Visit www.morefrommindy.com, for more information.

FOREWORD

Why are we so fascinated with the Amish? If we're not marveling at their enchanting dress and simple lifestyle, we're grappling with their unusual practices and austere ways. Our curiosity mingles with admiration, confusion, and suspicion. Just who are these people? Why do they live this way?

And why do we care so much?

Without a doubt, the Amish ignite our curiosity. We buy Amish-made products, cook Amish recipes, read Amish fiction. We take vacations to what we call "Amish country," those Amish-heavy regions like Lancaster County, Pennsylvania, and Holmes County, Ohio. While there, we look for them from our cars and think about sneaking photographs of them from a distance. We wonder what it would be like to live without constant interruptions, the stress of the rat race, and the intrusions of modern technology. Once in a while, we think we might like to be one of them, to live as they do.

Usually, those thoughts pass just as quickly as they

come, for we know we couldn't survive without television, without e-mail, without driving. We don't really want to be one of them, and yet the allure remains. The Amish themselves don't always understand our attraction either, but in response a wise Amish man once issued the following challenge:

> If you admire our faith, strengthen yours.
>
> If you admire our sense of commitment, deepen yours.
>
> If you admire our community spirit, build one.
>
> If you admire the simple life, cut back.
>
> If you admire quality merchandise or land stewardship, then make quality.
>
> If you admire deep character and enduring values, live them.

This popular saying is frequently posted on the walls of restaurants and tourist attractions in Amish country. The first time I saw it, I understood why its message was so important: We can't all be Amish, but in many ways, we would do well to follow their example.

Unfortunately, that's not always easy to do. Given the vast proliferation of Amish-related myths, inaccuracies, and outright fallacies, it's easy to misunderstand even the most basic facts about the Amish. The goal of this pocket guide is to clear up most of those misconceptions by providing accurate information about the Amish and the lives they lead in a thorough and easy-to-access format.

You'll notice some symbols in the text:

These *Fascinating Facts* about the Amish are particularly interesting and may be new to you.

These statements of *Takeaway Value* point out various Amish practices that we would do well to learn from and apply to our own lives.

These explanations of complicated concepts invite you to pause and *Think About It*.

These items show *The Flip Side*—a balanced view, both positive and negative, of a particular Amish value or practice.

These *In Their Own Words* quotes are taken directly from conversations and interviews with Amish men, women, and children.

These *Website Extras* indicate that more in-depth information is available at www.morefrommindy.com.

Living near Lancaster County myself, I have developed great respect for the Amish over the years. Though I could never live the life they live, I understand why it works for them. I do not see them through rose-colored glasses, nor do I pass judgment on their more incomprehensible regulations. The subject is so complex, in fact, that for this book I have chosen simply to observe, question, read, study, watch, interview, and report. This process has confirmed that the Amish way of life is utterly foreign to my own, the choices they make are unique, and their ways are genuinely worthy of study.

As you read and use this book, I hope that you will gain a deeper understanding of the Amish faith, life, and values, and that this will help you to form your own opinions about why you find them so intriguing. Most of all, my prayer is that you will use the Takeaway Value points from this knowledge to enhance your own faith. Thus, may we all be "iron sharpening iron"—Amish, author, and reader—helping each other to grow through a new perspective.

Enjoy!

PART ONE:

FOUNDATION

At long last, the day of the barn raising arrived with blue skies, a gentle breeze, and not a single cloud in sight. By dawn, a few cars and a steady stream of buggies had pulled up their lane. Matthew directed newcomers as to where to park and where to tie up horses. Several round hay stanchions had been set up where horses could eat their fill all day. Henry also carried buckets of water for the equine guests.

No one knew how many people would show up, but by seven o'clock at least two hundred were already milling around the Miller farm. More would come as soon as chores or necessary errands were finished.

—MARY ELLIS, *A WIDOW'S HOPE*

1

What Amish Means

What does the word *Amish* mean? Here's what *Webster's New World College Dictionary* says:

Am·ish (äm´is/h, am´-, ām´-)

plural noun
the members of a Christian sect that separated from the Mennonites in the 17th cent.: in the U.S. since the 18th cent., the Amish favor plain dress and plain living, with little reliance on modern conveniences, in a chiefly agrarian society

Etymology: after Jacob *Ammann* (or *Amen*), the founder

adjective
designating or of this sect

Of course, this definition doesn't even hint at the challenge of classifying this particular people group. Thanks to several centuries of church growth, expansion, and division, more than 25 different Amish affiliations exist in North America. These affiliations are further divided into approximately 1700 church districts. Amish settlements are located in 27 states and in Canada.

With no central religious authority, each Amish district must make decisions about what is and isn't allowed for its members on matters both large and small. Consequently, what may be perfectly permissible in one Amish district can be utterly forbidden in another. Outsiders might consider all Amish to be conservative, but that conservativism covers a wide range.

In Their Own Words

"For the Amish, culture and religion are intertwined to the point where it is hard to separate the two. Indeed, it is a faith culture."

Sweeping generalizations about the Amish are usually not helpful because of the myriad of differences between the various groups and subgroups. Every definitive statement seems to have an exception. We can begin to make sense of all of these variations by looking at the most obvious similarities and differences between the many groups who call themselves Amish.

Most Amish groups share these similarities:

- They adhere to a statement of faith known as the Eighteen Articles.

- They wear some form of distinctive "plain" clothing.

- They worship in each others' homes rather than in church buildings.

- They do not connect their houses with public utilities.

- They use horses and buggies as their primary means of transportation.

- They limit formal education to the eighth grade.

- They live in rural areas.

- They emphasize an agrarian lifestyle.

- They are pacifists.

- They choose their religious leaders through divine appointment by drawing lots.

- They speak a German dialect as their primary language.

- They value the history of their people and their martyrs' heritage.

On the other hand, Amish groups interpret and practice some of these distinctives in various ways. They also differ on many other items, including these:

technology

clothing

carriage styles

church discipline

plumbing

government assistance

facial hair

lawnmowers

transportation

assurance of salvation

The Focus of This Pocket Guide

To keep this book a manageable size, I have chosen to focus primarily on the largest and most well-known affiliation, the Old Order Amish. To avoid definitive statements that do not hold true for all Amish affiliations, or even for all Old Order districts, I use words like *usually* and *most* and *many* whenever describing Amish life and regulations. If you are seeking more extensive information, particularly on one of the less conservative groups, such as the Beachy Amish, or more conservative groups, such as the Swartzentruber, be sure to visit www.morefrommindy.com, which provides helpful resources for further study.

Finally, though the Amish have terms to describe those who are not Amish—such as *English* or *fancy*—I will most often use *non-Amish* and *outsider*. These seem appropriate because this guide is looking in on Amish life from the outside.

Fascinating Fact

The Amish call the non-Amish *English* because we speak English as our primary language instead of the German dialect they use.

The Word *Amish*

The word *Amish* originally referred to a group of conservative Christians who followed the teachings of a man named Jakob Ammann. Over the years, of course, *Amish* has grown to mean much more—including a faith culture, a way of life, a set of values, a style of clothing, and a collection of technological adaptations—becoming both a proper noun and an adjective.

These days, *Amish* is also a marketing buzzword and can be seen on everything from jars of jam to space heaters to backyard sheds and swing sets. Some outsiders use the Amish moniker to cash in on a reputation for quality, value, and integrity. Exploitative or not, those implications provide high praise to the ones who bear its title and live out its principles day after hardworking day.

2

BELIEFS

Some of the biggest misconceptions about the Amish have to do with their belief system. Are they a cult? Do they deny themselves modern comforts to earn their way into heaven? Do they even believe in the concept of salvation?

The Amish are Christians and adhere to these tenets of the Christian faith:

> There is one God.
>
> God is a trinity.
>
> Jesus came to earth as God in the flesh, died, and rose again.
>
> Salvation comes through grace by faith.
>
> Scripture is the divinely inspired word of God.
>
> The church is the body of Christ.

As foreign as many Amish practices are to most

people, their faith culture is a Christian one. The Amish are not a cult, they do not try to earn grace by their lifestyle, and they do believe in salvation.

Feeling that it would be prideful to claim an assurance of that salvation, however, most Amish districts prefer that their members maintain what they call a "living hope" or a "continued effort" on the topic, trusting the ultimate fate of their soul to God's providence rather than claiming it with certainty.

In Their Own Words

"The nice thing is that anyone can choose to be a follower of Christ regardless of his lot in life and the cultural context he lives in. No need to be Amish in order to believe in the Lord and have eternal life—unless, of course, the Lord wants you to be Amish."

Otherwise, most elements of the Amish lifestyle that seem unique or confusing relate not to some complicated or controversial theology but instead to the way they have chosen to live out their Christian walk in their day-to-day lives. They attempt to follow the teachings of Jesus, particularly the Sermon on the Mount, by emphasizing certain values. Though outsiders may think the Amish take some of these principles to the extreme, the tenets of their faith are based on the Bible.

Amish Values

To best understand Amish life, it helps to grasp the basic values that guide almost every facet of their faith. The Amish...

- *surrender* the self-will to God

- *submit* to authority, to the faith community, and to its rules

- *separate* from the world and become a "peculiar people" by turning to family and the faith community, by honoring history and tradition, and by turning the other cheek

- *simplify* through the practice of humility, modesty, thrift, and peacefulness

Jesus lived surrender, submission, separation, and simplicity throughout his life and thus provided the perfect example of these values in action. Even the night before he was crucified, he knelt in the garden of Gethsemane and prayed, "Remove this cup from me: nevertheless not my will, but thine, be done" (Luke 22:42 KJV). The Amish frequently cite this passage as the basis for trying to be as obedient in every area of life as Jesus was in that moment. Their many unique lifestyle regulations are based on this overriding goal of Christlikeness.

Takeaway Value

We should strive for Christlikeness in all that we do, even if in practice that may look different for us than it does for the Amish.

In Their Own Words

"All things considered, I think it is best to simply seek to do the Lord's will and follow his plan for my life. I was born in 1965 in Lancaster, Pennsylvania, to a specific set of Amish parents, and that was not an accident but rather part of a plan."

3

COMMUNITY

The community is the cornerstone of Amish life. It is where they most often find their identity, support, lifestyle, worship, classmates, spouses, and friends. It is a source of strength, an insurance policy when disaster strikes, and a safe haven in an often hostile (or at least intrusively curious) world.

To the outsider, this strong sense of community is one of the most appealing aspects of Amish life. Who wouldn't want the safety net of a loving group of friends and relatives to surround them during bad times, celebrate together in good times, and bear the ups and downs of life together? The very thought sounds like music to our culturally isolated ears. But then we consider the downside of Amish community: the myriad of rules that seem to constrict at every turn, the sacrificing of individuality for the greater good, the practices of excommunication and shunning that seem harsh and cruel. Would it be worth it? Could the benefits even exist without the drawbacks?

These elements of the Amish mind-set will help us understand the Amish view of community:

- Everyone in the community is accountable to God.
- The virtue of humility is shown through respect for God and others.
- All persons are worthy of dignity and respect.
- Communities are made stronger when individuals do not use personal desire as their supreme criteria for making decisions.
- Traditions are more important than progress.
- Accumulated wisdom is better than an individual's ideas.
- Authority in all of its various forms is to be obeyed. Ministers submit to bishops, members to leaders, wives to husbands, children to parents, students to teachers, younger to elder, and so on.

These beliefs help us understand why community is so important in Amish life.

Mutual Aid

In general, the Amish do not purchase commercial

insurance coverage, believing instead that when difficulty or disaster strikes, the church community members are to step in and help. This principle serves dual purposes: It helps keep the church separate from the world, and it binds the Amish community together and forces them to depend more heavily on each other. Some Amish communities have organized their own official insurance programs, though others handle members' needs on a less formal basis. In either case, the community provides care for members in need both physically and financially. For example…

- When members face large hospital bills that they cannot afford, the community pays the bills for them.

- When a building burns down, the community erects a new one.

- When someone dies, the community steps in to help with the funeral arrangements and takes over all farm and household chores for several days.

- When another community suffers a natural disaster, the community travels to that community to help.

- When a farmer is injured, the community takes over his farm work until he gets better.

Working Together

More hands make lighter work, or so the saying goes. The Amish have this principle down to a science and frequently share the load when doing tedious tasks. For example, adult sisters often meet once a month at each other's houses for what they call a *frolic*, which is simply a gathering together to visit with each other while doing chores such as canning food, shucking corn, cleaning house, and more. By rotating houses, they help each other out, get their own work done, and have fun all at the same time. Amish women also gather together for quilting parties, as they have for many years.

Perhaps the biggest symbol of community in action is the well-known Amish barn raising. These events involve hundreds of Amish working together for a single day. In about nine hours, they can construct an oak beam-and-peg barn that will last for generations. The Amish use their barns for farmwork, storing feed and grain, sheltering livestock, and housing valuable farm tools. Barns are also social centers where church services, funerals, marriages, and baptisms may be held.

To the outsider, the extent to which members of the Amish community care for each other is often mind-boggling. To the Amish, it is simply one of the primary values that define their lives.

The Flip Side

The good: Surrounded by a community of believers, one can always find friendship, fellowship, comfort, help, accountability, and more.

The bad: Such a tightly knit, mutually accountable arrangement can lead to nosiness, quick leaps to judgment, and gossip.

Takeaway Value

The idea of a work frolic is a great one whether you're Amish or not! Consider joining together with a group of friends or relatives once a month to spend a few hours doing tedious household chores and visiting as you work. The jobs will get done faster, and you'll enjoy a great visit at the same time. Rotate to a different house each month so everyone's home gets a turn.

4

SEPARATION

One of the core elements of the Amish faith is that Christians are to be *in* the world but not *of* the world. Many Amish practices are based on this principle, both in the ways they separate themselves from their non-Amish surroundings and in the ways they turn toward each other as a faith community.

The Biblical Foundation

Romans 12:2 instructs, "Do not conform any longer to the pattern of this world, but be transformed by the renewing of your mind." The Amish interpret verses like this to mean that they are to be different from the world in all parts of their lives—not only in thought but also in appearance and actions.

Persecution

We will see in chapter 11 that many of the early Anabaptists suffered persecution, torture, and death because of their beliefs, creating the "martyr tradition" on which the Amish faith was founded.

The Amish frequently revisit their tragic history in sermons, reading material, and even everyday conversation. A common feature in many Amish homes is the popular *Martyrs Mirror*, an 1100-page book that provides gruesome, detailed etchings and stories of many martyrs of the Christian faith. The Amish have suffered other periods of persecution through the years, though not as heinous as those acts committed against the Anabaptists in the sixteenth century. Their status as pacifist conscientious objectors, for example, made them easy targets for bullying, derision, and other kinds of torment in wartime America.

Though general sentiments toward the Amish have drastically changed over the years, this history of persecution nevertheless reinforced the Amish belief in a necessary division between the kingdoms of this world, which use laws and violence and coercion, and the kingdom of God, which is peaceful, loving, and kind.

Tangible Signs of Separation

The Amish convey their separation from society through specific acts both large and small, such as these:

- no electrical or telephone lines to Amish homes, as that would physically connect them with the outside world

- a unique style of dress, transportation, and other cultural markers that identify them as a unified group while also demonstrating their separation from the world

- limits on certain kinds of technology that may have a negative impact on the Amish home or church

- a directive to settle conflicts between believers within the structure of the church rather than the legal system or the government

- limits on outside monetary dependence such as commercial insurance coverage

When examining a particular peculiarity of the Amish lifestyle, viewing it in the light of their determination to remain separate from the world often helps make sense of confusing, seemingly arbitrary rules and regulations.

Fascinating Fact

Though the Amish don't have telephones in their homes, most do have access to a phone nearby. Often, several neighbors will share a single phone line that connects to a phone booth in a central location. This way, they are able to keep frivolous calls to a minimum, prevent disruptions to family time, and keep their homes "off the grid" while still having access to telephone service.

Taxes

The Amish pay all taxes that the non-Amish do, including income tax, property tax, sales tax, estate tax, and more. The only taxes from which they can choose to be exempt for religious purposes are Social Security and, in some states, workers' compensation. The Amish view both programs as forms of insurance, in which they generally do not participate. Instead, they prefer to follow the biblical directive to provide financially for each other in times of crisis rather than accept money from the government.

Insiders and Outsiders

By keeping to themselves, the Amish find strength through solidarity for their way of life. Despite their edict to be separate, however, the Amish have friendships with the non-Amish. As one Amish man says, "We treasure friendships of all kinds provided that our respective identities are not challenged and ripped down." Amish businesses also interact with non-Amish businesses on a regular basis.

Think About It

Visible Amish symbols of their voluntary separation from the world can provide an extra safeguard against temptation and sin. For example, once an Amish man marries, he no longer shaves his beard but instead allows it to grow. The bushy beard combined with a shaved upper lip marks him as Amish and married in a way that cannot be hidden or denied. A non-Amish man might take off a wedding ring and pretend to be single for a night, but an Amish man cannot simply remove his beard to reinvent himself—at least, not if he wants to put it back on again before going home to his wife!

5

Nonresistance

The Amish do not allow the use of force in human relations, which means they usually do not serve in the military, practice self-defense, hold political office, work as police officers, file lawsuits, or serve on juries.

When the Amish are confronted with a civic law that conflicts with their religious beliefs, they follow the example of the apostles, who said, "We must obey God rather than men!" (Acts 5:29). This has put them into some very uncomfortable positions. In the United States, the Amish have conflicted with local, state, and federal governments over issues of education, military service, property zoning, child labor, Social Security, health care, photo identification, road safety, and more. In 1967, the National Amish Steering Committee was formed to provide a unified voice on legal issues involving state and federal governments.

By working through this committee and living under the American political system, which protects freedom of religion, the Amish have managed to carve out exceptions, work through negotiations, and establish understandings with the government. These agreements have allowed them to continue their lifestyle with relatively few compromises. In practice, that means that while people in some settlements may be required to display reflective triangles or tape on the backs of their buggies for safety purposes, they are also able to register as conscientious objectors, exempt themselves from Social Security, teach their children in their own private schools, and allow those children to complete their schooling at the end of the eighth grade.

The Flip Side

The good: The Amish follow the biblical directive to not take each other to court or parade conflicts between community members in front of nonbelievers.

The bad: By not always involving the police or courts in more serious matters, such as abuse or molestation, these situations can exist unchecked.

Takeaway Value

As Christians, we would do well to follow the Amish example of standing up in a nonviolent manner against laws and ordinances that violate our religious convictions and freedoms. More importantly, we should remember in prayer and deed our brothers and sisters in Christ in other parts of the world whose religious rights are never protected by law and who suffer tremendous persecution for their beliefs.

6

ORGANIZATION

Amish society is built on three units (besides, of course, the family): a *settlement*, which is a geographical division, a *district*, which is a congregational designation, and an *affiliation*, which is a lifestyle distinction.

A *settlement* is a cluster of Amish living within a common geographical area. Beliefs and practices can vary widely within a single settlement, particularly in those that are the most densely populated. (A settlement can have less than 100 people or more than 30,000.) The Young Center for Anabaptist and Pietist Studies estimates that as of July 2009, 423 settlements existed in the United States and Canada. The three largest settlements in the country are in Holmes County, Ohio; Lancaster County, Pennsylvania; and Elkhart/LaGrange, Indiana.

Fascinating Fact

The oldest surviving Amish settlement is in Lancaster County, Pennsylvania. The largest Amish settlement is in and around Holmes County, Ohio.

A *district* is a group of Amish who live near each other and worship together, somewhat like a congregation or a parish. Districts average about 135 people (20 to 40 families), and as membership and families grow, new districts are created by dividing existing districts.

Old Order Amish usually have no church buildings, choosing instead to hold services and other functions in each others' homes or barns. Thus, dividing into districts is necessary so that members can continue to meet within homes and so that all Amish congregations within a settlement remain relatively similar in size. District boundaries are usually defined along geographical markers such as streams and roads, and in more densely populated Amish settlements, it is not unusual for across-the-street neighbors (even if they are close relatives) to belong to completely different districts. The Young Center estimates that as of July 2009, the United States and Canada contained 1727 districts.

Think About It

Limiting a district's size serves a number of practical purposes, but it carries with it a spiritual component as well. Ever notice that there are no Old Order Amish megachurches? Keeping the districts small maintains spiritual intimacy. It also prevents any one district from becoming too powerful or, more importantly, too prideful.

An *affiliation* is a collection of districts with similar lifestyle regulations and cooperative relationships among their leaders. Affiliations are not defined by geography but by practices and beliefs. Roughly 25 different Amish affiliations exist in the United States and Canada.

As long as they are in the same affiliation, members of different districts can fellowship, attend each others' church services, intermarry, and even exchange ministers and share bishops. Though rules and practices may vary somewhat from district to district, the districts in an affiliation follow practices and beliefs that are similar enough to allow interaction.

The bishops in an affiliation meet together regularly to discuss issues and look for common stances. This provides unity within the affiliation and support for the bishops as they administer their districts.

Think About It

Unlike many religious denominations, the Amish have no central authority—no pope, synod, convention, diocese, association, or the like. Instead, the ultimate authority for Amish life and practice lies within each local district. This is why rules can vary from district to district even within an affiliation—each congregation follows the rules established by its own leaders.

7

LEADERSHIP

Amish church leadership includes three positions: bishop, minister, and deacon. These leaders serve at the district level, which is where the ultimate authority lies within the Amish faith. They work individually and together to guide the actions of their district.

Bishops

The primary spiritual leader of the district is the bishop. Most bishops serve one district, except in Lancaster County, where one bishop usually serves two districts. These are some of the bishop's duties:

- conduct congregational meetings, baptisms, communions, weddings, ordinations, and funerals

- interpret and enforce district regulations

- resolve matters of disobedience, discipline, and dispute

- recommend excommunication or reinstatement when necessary
- serve as interim bishop to neighboring districts when needed
- preach in some Sunday services

Most experts consider the Amish to be a "patriarchal democracy." When a decision needs to be made, the bishop gives a recommendation, and the congregation votes on it. Though church leaders are always male, the women of the church participate in the voting processes and in the nomination of leaders.

Ministers

Under the bishop are the ministers, or preachers. Most districts have two or three ministers, whose duties include preaching in services and assisting the bishop by serving the congregation in various ways.

Deacons

Most districts have one deacon, who performs duties like these:

- read Scripture or recite prayer in worship services
- supervise the financial aid of the church
- assist with baptisms and communion

- investigate rule violations in the congregation

- deliver news of excommunication or reinstatement to parties involved

- serve as the church's representative in the facilitation of marriages

Selection Process

The process for choosing leaders in the Amish church is based on "divine appointment" through the drawing of lots, as shown in Acts 1:24-26.

The Amish choose their potential ministers and deacons by nominating candidates from among its male members of the congregation. Nominees who receive the required number of votes then draw lots. (Bishops are also chosen by lot, though nominees come from among the eligible ministers rather than the congregation at large.)

Leaders have no formal theological training, and they serve for life without financial remuneration. They spend a lot of time and effort on their duties, employing diplomacy, dealing with difficult issues, and sometimes making unpopular decisions that impact the entire group. Thus, despite the honor of being nominated, many dedicated, godly Amish men prefer *not* to be chosen as a leader. The amount of time and energy required to fulfill their leadership commitments can have a negative impact on their work and farms. Still, most accept the mantle with grace, following the example of Christ in saying, "Not my will, but thine, be done" (Luke 22:42 KJV).

Fascinating Fact

The choosing of lots is usually done on a communion Sunday. A Bible verse is written on a piece of paper and then hidden inside a hymnbook. That hymnbook is mixed with several others, and each nominee chooses one. The man who chooses the hymnbook that has the verse inside is the new leader.

In Their Own Words

"The fact that ministers are chosen from among the members by the use of the divine lot eliminates a great deal of politics, a fact that I personally greatly appreciate."

8

WORSHIP

Amish worship services are usually held every other Sunday and rotate among the homes in a district. If a house is not large enough to accommodate the entire congregation, a service may be held in a barn, a basement, or a large shop. Each Amish family hosts the service about once a year, depending on the size of the district. For congregational seating, the district provides hard, wooden-backed benches that are delivered to the host home the day before on a special wagon that has been designed for just that purpose.

In the service, which lasts about three hours, the congregation is usually divided by gender and age. Very young children sit with a parent. From the youngest to the oldest, everyone is expected to sit still and pay attention despite several challenges: the length of the service; the use of the less-familiar High German in the songs, prayers, and readings; the hard wooden benches; and any seasonal discomfort, such as summer heat or winter chill.

Old Order worship services generally open with a hymn sung slowly, in unison, without instruments, in High German. As the congregation sings, the bishop and ministers gather in a different room and decide who will preach the opening sermon and who will preach the main sermon. Besides congregational singing, services feature Scripture reading in High German, silent prayer, and spoken prayer read from a prayer book, also in High German.

The opening sermon, given in the Pennsylvania Dutch dialect without the aid of any notes, lasts 20 to 30 minutes. This is followed by the main sermon, which lasts an hour or more and is also given extemporaneously.

Sometimes, "the preaching experience itself can be quite powerful," relates author Erik Wesner on his blog, Amish America. "Just as among the English, different preachers have different styles. Some rely on repetition to make their points. Others become visibly emotional. I recall a sermon I was witness to in Ohio. Though I had difficulty understanding the Pennsylvania Dutch, it was obvious that the preacher was visibly moved by his message, becoming teary-eyed at one point."

When the main sermon is over, other ministers may add input or correction as they feel led. In general, services avoid formal theology, instead focusing on practical applications of obedience, humility, faith, community, and simplicity. The church service is often followed by a light communal meal. For dining, some of the wooden benches are stacked and used as tables.

Because church is held every other Sunday, on the alternating Sundays the Amish may spend quiet family time at home, gather with others for informal readings from the King James Version of the Bible, or attend the services of a different district in their affiliation. No work is done on Sundays except that which is absolutely necessary, such as the care and feeding of the animals.

Communion Day

Twice a year, in spring and fall, the Amish hold a special communion service that includes foot washing. This event is preceded by a council meeting, concludes with an offering of alms for the needy, and can last eight hours!

Think About It

Old Order Amish rarely deal with discussions or teachings of formal theology in the church, home, or school. They have no Sunday school or training union, no children's programs, and no youth retreats. Some formal religious training is provided prior to baptism. Otherwise, instead of concerning themselves with theology, their emphasis is on the practice of faith in action through surrender, submission, separation, and simplicity in their day-to-day lives. As the Amish saying goes, "Learn obedience first, and the rest will follow."

9

RULES

The Amish believe that setting limits and respecting them are keys to Christlikeness, wisdom, and fulfillment. To them, regulations shape identity, build community, help prevent temptation, and provide a sense of belonging. Without rules, they feel, one can fall prey to pride, unhappiness, insecurity, loss of dignity, and ultimately self-destruction.

Limitations on Amish life are dictated by the *Ordnung*, which is what the Amish call the unwritten set of rules and regulations that dictates their day-to-day life. The *Ordnung* deals with a wide variety of topics, such as clothing, transportation, technology, education, and much more.

Rules in the *Ordnung* can vary widely from affiliation to affiliation and can even vary somewhat from district to district within the same affiliation. As districts grow and divide into new ones and as new technologies and issues arise, the *Ordnung* necessarily changes and adapts as well. Minor regulations are updated by church leaders as needed, but major decisions usually involve congregational input and can cause debate in member meetings.

Regardless of how intensely various issues are debated, all matters of contention are laid to rest at the twice-yearly council meetings that precede the communion services. Once the group is at peace with each other and the rules, members reaffirm the commitment they made when they were first baptized to follow the *Ordnung*. In this way, they remain united as a people.

Think About It

Passed along through an oral tradition, the *Ordnung* by necessity changes and evolves with every new issue that arises and every new technology that presents itself for consideration. When deciding whether something should be allowed, church leaders focus on key questions like these:

Will this force us to be more connected to the outside world?

Will this create division in our families?

Will this take us too far from home?

For example, members of some Old Order communities do not have bicycles. After all, if one has a bicycle, he or she may take too much time away from home and family or venture into the outside world too fully. Thus, with an eye toward the what-ifs of the situation, a decision is made for the district and becomes a part of its *Ordnung*.

In Their Own Words

"Sometimes we do agree to look the other way. For lesser things that are frowned upon, like smoking or hanging up decorations, well, those things are just kind of 'tolerated,' so to speak, in the interest of community harmony."

10

DISCIPLINE

Baptism into the Amish faith is an intentional, voluntary, adult act that requires a tremendous commitment. In the baptism ceremony, candidates vow to obey God and the church for the rest of their lives. This is an act of submission that binds them under the rules of the *Ordnung*. Once this commitment has been made, any infraction of those rules is subject to church discipline, whether the infraction is minor (such as using forbidden technology) or major (such as committing adultery).

The discipline process is careful and deliberate and usually begins with a reprimand from a church elder that is intended to bring reconciliation and repentance. If the disobedient member discontinues his infractions, confesses, and repents, all is forgiven, and he remains within good standing in the fold. If he continues in sin or gives up the sin but remains unrepentant, he is put on temporary probation.

During the probationary period, repeated attempts

are made to help him see the error of his ways. Elders, friends, and family will talk with him, pray for him, and remind him that he is not living in submission to church authority as he vowed to do when he was baptized. Many attempts are made toward reconciliation, and often this is enough to turn the most stubborn heart toward confession and repentance.

When this is not the case, more drastic steps are taken. If the bishop recommends excommunication, the members will vote. If the vote passes, the person is excommunicated, or put under the *ban*. In most districts, excommunication is followed by what the Amish call *Meidung*, or shunning, though the severity of the shunning can vary widely from district to district.

In Their Own Words

"Shunning is usually done with great reluctance and only once there is nothing else left to do. Upon repentance the relationship is restored, and what is in the past stays in the past."

The practice of shunning is one of the most well-known facets of Amish life. Unfortunately, it's also one of the most misunderstood. Though it seems cruel to outsiders, shunning is actually considered to be an act of love, one that is biblically based and done out of concern for the sinner. The Amish stress several key points about shunning:

- Those who have never been baptized into the church are not subject to excommunication or shunning. (See chapters 20 and 21, "*Rumspringa*" and "*Baptism*," for more information.)

- Baptism and its accompanying commitment to honor the *Ordnung* and submit to the authority of the church is made voluntarily, not under duress, and as an adult, not as a child. As such, the candidate accepts from day one that any future infractions of the *Ordnung* will incur discipline.

- When people are shunned, the door is always open for them to return, as long as they are willing to confess and repent.

- When a person who has been shunned returns to the fold and confesses with a contrite heart, all is forgiven, the relationship is restored, and, as one Amish man says, "The past is left in the past."

Shunning is painful both for the one who is shunned and the ones who are doing the shunning, particularly the closest family members. In its strictest form, called *Streng Meidung,* members in good standing cannot dine at the same table with those who are shunned, nor can they accept rides or gifts from them or conduct business transactions. When one member of a married couple is shunned, the spouse in good standing may not sleep in the same bed or have marital relations. Conversation is sometimes allowed, but a definite line is drawn between the one who is under the ban and the rest of the community.

Those who have been shunned and eventually leave the church often describe the experience as unspeakably cruel, yet those who have been shunned but eventually repent and return to the fold are often grateful for the experience, saying it was difficult but in the end brought them closer to Christ and to the church.

Regardless of how you feel about the topic, the fact remains that shunning is often an effective method for bringing about repentance. When that doesn't happen, at least it helps keep the membership free from those who are not willing to follow the rules. The apostle Paul gives a precedent in 1 Corinthians 5:11-13, where he admonishes the Corinthian Christians, "Expel the wicked man from among you." As Wesner says, shunning is "tough love on a community-wide scale."

The Flip Side

The good: Once a matter is confessed and forgiven, it is also supposed to be forgotten. This new start with a clean slate makes for less baggage for all and can be the best way to move forward after an issue has been resolved.

The bad: Many Amish can be somewhat naive about the principle of repentance. The forgive-and-forget mentality is applied even to the most serious of offenses, but without legal safeguards, even the most sincere of confessors can become repeat offenders. Such was the case with Mary Byler, an Amish girl who was the victim in the largest incidence of sexual assault in Amish American history. More than once, her rapists confessed and repented, only to commit the same atrocities soon thereafter.

Abuse is no more common among the Amish than in the general population, but where it does exist, forgiving and forgetting can create an environment for continued reoccurance.

11

HISTORY

The roots of the Amish faith trace back to the Protestant Reformation of the early sixteenth century. The Anabaptist movement began in Switzerland with a small group of Christians who began to question certain practices of the church, including the deep intertwining of church and state and the rite of infant baptism. They felt that baptism should be reserved for adults who have made a voluntary, conscious decision to follow Christ, not for children who have no understanding or consent. They also objected to financial and regulatory dealings of the church as they related to the Swiss government.

In 1525, things came to a head when this group was ordered by the city council of Zurich to baptize their infants. In response, the men of the group baptized each other instead. Because they had all been baptized previously as infants, they became known as "rebaptizers" or Anabaptists. They formed the first church of the Radical Reformation and began evangelizing despite numerous arrests and other government interference. Civil officials and religious leaders were further infuriated at the Anabaptist insistence that religious preference should be voluntary and free from government oversight.

The Anabaptist movement gained strength and spread so rapidly that within a year the Zurich city council passed an edict that made adult baptism a crime punishable by death. On January 5, 1527, an Anabaptist evangelist named Felix Manz was executed, making him one of the first Swiss Anabaptists to be martyred. Another hero of the Anabaptist faith was Menno Simons, a Franciscan priest who left Catholicism to become an Anabaptist in 1536. Simons was a wise and influential leader, and his followers became known as the Mennonites.

Between 1550 and 1625, more than 2500 Anabaptists were killed for their beliefs, often in horrific, tortuous ways. In response, they were forced to go underground and into rural areas to hide, with their meetings held in homes, barns, boats, and other private places. Some Mennonites immigrated to the Alsatian region of France to avoid persecution and compulsory military service.

In 1693, one of these immigrants, a leader in the Mennonite church named Jakob Ammann, proposed a number of changes to the Mennonite faith, including these:

- Communion should be held twice a year and should include foot washing.

- To ensure doctrinal purity and spiritual discipline, congregational regulations should be enforced.

- Members who were excommunicated should be shunned.

Ammann's beliefs and practices eventually caused a split among the Mennonites, and those who followed Ammann became known as the Amish.

Coming to America

The first American Amish settlements were begun in Berks County, Pennsylvania, in the 1730s. In 1737, a ship called the *Charming Nancy* sailed to America with 21 Amish families on board. More Amish followed in the years to come, and in the mid to late 1700s, the early colonies of the present-day Lancaster County settlement were established.

A second wave of Amish immigration began in 1815, when about 3000 adults surged into North America. Though many of these immigrants first came to Pennsylvania, most of them moved on to other states, particularly Ohio, Illinois, Indiana, Iowa, and New York, as well as Ontario. By the mid 1800s, Amish settlements were dotted across the country, and leaders were struggling to find compromises and solutions in disputes about various Amish regulations.

Internal disagreements and divisions would plague the Amish church for many years despite earnest attempts to resolve differences. Groups that found themselves at impasses over nonnegotiable points sometimes split and formed new affiliations. The Old Order Amish were formed this way in 1865, followed by a number of other groups, including the Peachy Amish (later called the Beachy Amish) in 1909.

From the 1920s to the early 1970s, the Amish also struggled against the U.S. government, primarily in matters dealing with nonresistance and education. See chapter 19, "School," for more information about *Wisconsin v. Yoder*, the 1972 landmark decision of the U.S. Supreme Court that allowed Amish communities educational leeway under their right to freedom of religion.

Changing Perceptions

In the years that followed that Supreme Court decision, a new attitude about the Amish began to emerge. Suspicion gave way to compassion and curiosity, especially as time passed and ill feelings engendered during the World Wars over the Amish stance on nonresistance faded into the background. As *diversity* and *tolerance* became American buzzwords, the Amish gained a new level of acceptance.

The days of blatant Amish persecution and ostracism may be gone, but now the Amish face a whole new set of problems as the pendulum has swung to the opposite extreme. With such a wide acceptance of and curiosity about the Amish, an entire branch of the tourism industry has developed, bringing with it overcrowding, intrusiveness, rising land costs, and outright exploitation. See chapter 24, "Tourism and Media," for more information.

Website Extra

Visit www.morefrommindy.com for more information about how modern perceptions of Amish life have changed in the past few decades.

12

EXPANSION

According to current estimates, the Amish population doubles about every 20 years. Growth is propelled by two factors:

- Birth rate—the average Amish family has seven children.
- Retention rate—fully 85 percent of those Amish children choose to join the church when they become adults.

Future projections for Amish population growth vary widely, but most experts say this growth rate shows no signs of slowing anytime soon.

Hitting the Road

Many Amish are choosing to leave established communities and head to new areas, usually in search of available and affordable farmland. This is especially the case in Lancaster County, where family farms have been divided and subdivided over the years, and most have reached their limits and can be divided no further. Even when new land is available, prices have climbed so high that young farmers cannot afford to purchase large tracts.

Some Amish families are migrating out of the more populous settlements for other reasons as well, such as...

excessive tourism

zoning and other municipal issues

weak economies and changes in the job market

disagreements with a church district

When choosing a destination, the Amish consider criteria such as these:

lower land prices

fertile soil and good farming climate

occupational opportunities

proximity to family or other Amish

proximity to similar districts within an affiliation

neighbors' acceptance of the Amish and their ways

Migrating Amish may join an established settlement or start a new one from scratch.

Think About It

The Amish do allow converts to their faith, though successful, permanent conversions of outsiders into the Amish faith are extremely rare. At first glance, one might assume that the reason for this is the difficult nature of the Amish life. The hard work of farming, the lack of technology, the need for frugality—these would all be incredibly difficult adjustments, especially for one who has grown up in a world of relative luxury and modern conveniences. Becoming Amish would mean not only giving up things like computers, telephones, and electricity but also changing one's ways of doing almost everything from heating a home to educating children to cooking dinner. The adjustment would be exhausting.

The physical struggle, however, might in fact be the easier part of the transition. Far more difficult must be the internal adjustments required, the reframing of thought, the achievement of the Amish mentality. From a very young age, the Amish are taught that one must continually die to self, resist pride at all costs, and often place greater good over personal desires. Their goal is to live in constant obedience and submission—to God, to their church leaders, to each other.

For the average person living in a postmodern world, the thought of sacrificing personal identity for the greater good is foreign indeed. Encouraged at a young age to stand out from the crowd and to be proud of our accomplishments, we learn to celebrate individuality, creativity, and personal freedom. Eschewing these things for the Amish frame of mind would be difficult if not nearly impossible for anyone who was not raised in that culture.

PART TWO:
LIFESTYLE

I was astounded at the sheer quantity of food that was heaped upon platters on the table: pork chops in sauerkraut, homemade bread, noodles in butter, and a variety of vegetables that the family had likely grown and canned themselves. After a silent prayer, everyone dug in, and even the women scooped up generous portions of butter for their bread.

The meal passed so pleasantly that about halfway through I simply allowed myself to sit there and take it all in. How could I have forgotten what it was like to be in an Amish kitchen and listen to the gentle banter, the politeness of the children, the sweet teasing of the husband and wife?

—MINDY STARNS CLARK,
SHADOWS OF LANCASTER COUNTY

13

CLOTHING AND GROOMING

The Amish follow established rules regarding their appearance. Specifics vary between districts and affiliations, but almost all have rules that address head coverings, hairstyles, facial hair for men, clothing choices for males and females, and footwear. There are even clothing and grooming differences between those who are married and unmarried.

Having such a highly regulated manner of dress demonstrates submission to authority and provides a visible public symbol of group identity. Even outsiders who know nothing about the ways and values of the Amish can easily recognize them because of how they're dressed.

Christlikeness

The Amish emphasis on Christlikeness is expressed through clothing in several ways:

Humility: Dressing alike provides less opportunity for vanity.

Submission: Following the clothing rules of the

district demonstrates obedience to God, to the group, and to history.

Denial of self: Dressing alike prevents individuality and pride.

Simplicity: Limiting clothing choices saves time and effort.

Modesty: Prescribed styles guarantee propriety.

Thrift: Making clothes, especially from limited fabric and pattern choices, saves money, as does the lack of jewelry and clothing accessories.

Guidelines

Though specifics can vary from district to district, all Amish clothing is modest, loose fitting, and of a predetermined style and choice of colors. Clothing worn to church differs somewhat from that worn during the week. In some districts, buttons, collars, and lapels are taboo because they are too closely associated with military uniforms.

Head coverings are worn every day by men, women, and teens. Children wear head coverings in church and at school, though not always in more casual settings, depending on district rules.

Many Amish, both young and old, enjoy going barefoot much of the time. Shoes, when worn, may be lace-ups, slip-ons, or sneakers, depending on district rules, and are almost always dark.

In deference to 1 Corinthians 11:2-16, Amish women never cut their hair but instead allow it to grow. They consider a woman's hair to be her glory, which she shares only with her husband in private. Otherwise, Amish women part their hair in the middle, pull it tightly back, and fasten it into a bun or braid. Prayer coverings are worn over the hair. In general, the less conservative a district, the smaller the female's head covering.

Men

For everyday wear, Amish men usually sport dark broadfall trousers with a flap that buttons at the waist. These are worn with suspenders. In the interest of modesty, suspenders allow for a looser fit, and in the interest of humility, they supplant belt buckles, which are considered fancy.

Shirts are in prescribed colors only, and though Old Order Amish and other conservative groups do not allow plaids or stripes, some less conservative sects may. The most common approved shirt colors are those found in nature, including blue, green, brown, and maroon.

Men usually wear banded straw hats for work and chores, with the width of the brim and the height of the crown determined by district rules.

Black wool or felt hats are worn on the Sundays, along with black dress shoes, black suits, and white shirts. Suits include broadfall pants with suspenders, vests fastened with hooks and eyes, and coats, which may or may not have buttons or lapels, depending on district rules.

When not being worn, men's felt hats are kept in hat presses.

Once a man marries, he stops shaving his beard, though he continues to shave his mustache. (Like buttons and lapels, mustaches are forbidden because they are associated with the military.) In general, beards are not to be trimmed or neatened. Hair is worn blunt cut in a uniform style, usually no longer than collar length.

Women

For everyday wear and for church, women sport calf- to ankle-length dresses. The community determines a uniform style and set of colors, with the most common shades taken from nature. Over these full-skirted dresses go aprons and capes, usually black. Capes are made from a wide piece of fabric that is crossed in the front and comes to a point in the back. Straight pins are usually used in lieu of buttons to fasten the cape at the waist in front and back.

Women wear prayer coverings (also called *Kapps*) on their heads. Depending on district and marital status, these coverings may be white or black. They often cover the ears at least partially and have strings that may or may not be tied, also depending on district rules. In winter, a warmer bonnet of an approved design may be worn over the prayer cap.

Amish women often go barefoot at home. When worn, shoes are usually dark sneakers, lace-ups, or slip-ons (depending on regulations) and are worn with dark stockings.

Amish women sew most of the clothes for their family. Districts usually allow the use of modern synthetic fabrics as long as they are in the permitted range of colors. As girls grow up, they are taught to sew, and by their teenage years, they may be skilled enough to help outfit the entire family.

Neither jewelry nor makeup is allowed.

Children

For school, play, or chores, boys wear broadfall pants with suspenders and shirts in approved colors along with banded straw hats. For church, they wear black suits similar in style to those worn by the adults, along with black felt hats.

Girls usually wear solid-color jumpers in approved colors, topped by loose, pinafore-style white or black aprons.

Clothing Storage

In many Amish homes, clothing is stored on pegs along the wall. This illustration shows the clothes and hats in the boys' room of an Amish home.

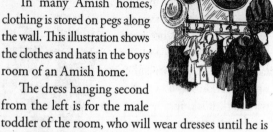

The dress hanging second from the left is for the male toddler of the room, who will wear dresses until he is potty trained, at which point he will "graduate" into the pants-and-shirt attire of his older brothers.

Takeaway Value

Though few of us would choose to limit our clothing options as severely as the Amish have, there is something to be said for the simplicity of the Amish way of dressing. Think about the amount of time you spend on clothing—shopping for it, coordinating outfits, cleaning it, storing it, finding the right shoes and the right accessories, and so on. Imagine, then, how it would feel to wake up and face a simple closet or row of clothing pegs, knowing that your only choice is between three colors of the same dress. Many days, I wish I could have such a streamlined wardrobe and spend my time on far more important matters!

In Their Own Words

"[My big brother is getting married in a few weeks, and] I'm waiting to see how fast his beard grows in. I think it'll happen right quick, not like my sister's husband. He's been married almost a year, and his is still just a scruffy little thing!"

14

LANGUAGE

Amish life involves three different languages: Pennsylvania Dutch, English, and High German.

Pennsylvania Dutch is the primary language of the Amish, spoken at home, in sermons at church, and among other Amish. Though other religious groups also spoke this German-derived American language in the past, the Amish and the Old Order Mennonites maintain it to the present day.

The language is based on a Palatine dialect that was brought to America from Germany in the 1700s, primarily by a mass influx of Lutherans and German Reformed Church members searching for religious freedom. Once here, their dialect began to mix with other dialects and with the English of the colonists, evolving into what eventually became known as Pennsylvania Dutch. Today, though the language's grammatical structures are still based on Palatine German, about 5 to 10 percent of the vocabulary comes from the English language.

In Indiana, a few Amish communities use a Swiss dialect for their primary language rather than Pennsylvania Dutch.

Fascinating Fact

A common misconception about Pennsylvania Dutch is that it is a variant of the Dutch language. This isn't true. The German word for *German* is *Deutsch*, which sounds a lot like *Dutch*, and one theory holds that over the years, the term for Pennsylvania German, or Pennsylvania *Deutsch*, began to be pronounced Pennsylvania Dutch.

English is the language of commerce, literacy, and the outside world.

The Amish are fluent in English and use the language when speaking with non-Amish friends, conducting business outside of the community, and functioning in other non-Amish settings. The Amish are taught to speak, read, and write English in school, and most continue to use it when writing throughout their lives.

Though many Amish speak English without any telltale accent, there are some giveaways when they talk, particularly among those who do not converse often with outsiders. Certain words and terms receive unusual pronunciations and uniquely Amish phraseology. There are many charming Amish English idioms, such as "The cookies are all but the milk is yet," which means "The cookies are all gone but some milk is still left."

For me, much of the fun of reading and writing Amish fiction is to pick up these peculiarities of Amish speech. Contrary to how they are often portrayed in the media, the Amish do not use archaic terms such as *thee* and *thou* when speaking English.

Think About It

Most Amish do not learn to speak English until they start school, a practice that helps insulate and protect them from outside influences for their first five to seven years.

High German is used in Amish worship services and spiritual texts. It is the language of respect for God and heritage. Most Amish become familiar with the language not through formal instruction but rather from years of exposure during Sunday worship and when reading the classics of the Amish faith that are in High German, including these:

- The *Ausbund*, or Amish hymnal, was first published in 1564. Many of its songs were written by martyrs of the faith in the sixteenth century. It is the oldest Christian songbook in continuous use.

- *Die Ernsthafte Christenpflicht* is a prayer book used in many Amish households.
- The Luther Bible.

The Amish value High German as an important symbol of their spiritual heritage.

15

TECHNOLOGY

The Amish are very selective about the technological devices and innovations that they possess or use. Most Amish do not have electricity in their homes. Some types of technology are permitted, but not televisions, radios, stereos, or personal computers. The Amish do not own cars.

Contrary to popular belief, the Amish do not think that technology itself is evil or wrong. They do believe, however, that if left unchecked, technology can destroy the Amish way of life by undermining its traditions, bringing inappropriate value systems into homes, and ultimately breaking communities and families apart.

Values

To the outsider, the Amish restrictions on technology are among the most confusing of their rules and often seem contradictory. Why do the Amish not own or drive cars, yet they will ride in vehicles driven by others? Why do they not use electricity, yet they will use other forms of power, such as propane and gasoline? Why won't they have a phone in the house but put one in the barn? To make sense of these questions and more, consider the Amish value system:

Humility: A lack of fancy electronic devices provides less opportunity for pride.

Submission: Following the technology rules of the order demonstrates obedience to God, to the group, and to history.

Community: Staying off the grid prevents dependence on the outside world.

Simplicity: Life without computers, e-mail, or other forms of electronic interruption is more peaceful.

Thrift: A low-tech life prevents excessive phone bills, car insurance premiums, cable TV charges, Internet costs, music download fees, and so on.

Family: Owning and driving one's own car provides too many opportunities for temptation and allows one to roam too far from home.

Rules that seem contradictory usually relate to the overriding goal of being masters over technology rather than slaves to it. Anyone who has ever felt prisoner to a constantly ringing phone or a full e-mail inbox can surely understand that concept!

Evaluating Technology

As explained in chapter 9, "Rules," when a new technology becomes available to a district, church leaders will evaluate its potential for causing harm to Amish life and values and then decide whether to allow it. No technology, regardless of how labor-saving it may be, is permissible if the leaders determine that it will be spiritually detrimental to the community.

Though the rules vary widely from district to district, many technological items are allowed in Amish homes and farms, including calculators, flashlights, manual typewriters, gas grills, chain saws, inline skates, and more. Some districts allow manual lawnmowers only, though others permit gas-powered lawnmowers and even weed whackers.

In many Amish homes and farms, other items are allowed as long as they have been adapted to work with non-electric fuel sources, such as propane or batteries. These include refrigerators, lights, shop tools, fans, copy machines, sewing machines, smoke alarms, some farm equipment, hot water heaters, washing machines, and more. Tractors often must be adapted for off-road use, lest they provide the opportunity to go too far from home. This usually means steel tires rather than rubber. In many communities, tractors are not used in the fields at all but instead may only be used inside or near the barn as sources for high-powered needs such as blowing silage to the top of silos, powering feed grinders and hydraulic systems, pumping liquid manure, and so on.

In most cases, hay balers can be used in the fields as long as they are pulled by horses rather than self-propelled.

Adaptations

In many districts, the Amish have adapted household technology so that it works with approved energy sources. Here is a sample of these adaptations:

- lanterns and lamps powered by kerosene, naphtha, gasoline, and propane
- stoves powered by wood, kerosene, bottled gas, or propane
- refrigerators powered by kerosene or propane
- small appliances powered by compressed air
- plumbing powered by wind, water, gas, diesel, compressed air, or gravity
- water heaters powered by wood, coal, kerosene, or bottled gas

- household heaters powered by wood, propane, or natural gas

- washing machines powered by compressed air or gasoline

Not all districts allow all types of power, but the Amish have found remarkably ingenious ways to make their lives easier using permissible power sources instead of hooking into the grid.

The Great Digital Debate

The greatest current technological threats to the Amish way of life are coming from the workplace. As more and more Amish leave farming behind and take up manufacturing and other jobs, they are exposed to computers, cell phones, and the Internet. To further complicate matters, many Amish-owned businesses, including farms, have felt compelled to enter the computer and cell-phone age as well. When the success or failure of a business depends on a device, leaders hesitate to draw the line and say it cannot be used— at least not hastily and without an enormous amount of thought and debate first.

Such was the case with the rules regarding tractors on farms. Starting as far back as the 1920s, leaders have faced tractor-related conundrums that have required much thought and careful decision making all along the way, especially with the release of each new type of tractor technology that has come along.

Unfortunately for the Amish, digital technology development races along at a speed far greater than that of mechanical tractor development. Until the districts draw a hard-and-fast line for or against the various types of digital technology, more and more Amish are gaining exposure to and experience with them. Cell phones are the biggest issue as they are used both by parents in the workplace and teens prior to baptism. One isn't likely to see a cell phone at an Amish dinner table anytime soon, but many are hidden in pockets or under pillows, waiting to be used in more private moments.

One Amish mother explains that she wouldn't have a problem with teens owning cell phones (as long as they didn't use them in the home), but she *is* concerned about the Internet access that her children would get through those cell phones.

Until a final decision is made, this quiet infiltration is likely to continue. On a recent trip to Lancaster County, I personally saw a sight that made me do a double take: an Amish youth, relaxing on a trampoline in his front yard, busily texting away with his thumbs just like any other American teenager.

Fascinating Fact

The Amish do not own cameras or take photographs, though this has nothing to do with restrictions on technology. Instead, the Amish believe that photographs are strictly prohibited by Exodus 20:4, which says, "You shall not make for yourself an idol in the form of anything in heaven above or on the earth beneath or in the waters below."

Takeaway Value

On a recent vacation to upstate New York, we stayed in a cottage near Lake Champlain. The place was surrounded by all sorts of opportunities for water sports, hiking, sightseeing, and more. When we arrived, I told my husband I was glad to see that the cottage had a television, as I had brought my Wii Fit just in case.

"*Wii* Fit?" he laughed. "How about we go outside and enjoy some *real* fit?"

It's easy to forget how "simulated" our lives are these days. Studying the Amish way of life reminds us that we can survive without all of the gadgets and devices that we think are so indispensible.

We also need to keep in mind technology's "dark side": cell phones that stop us from ever getting away from the office, texting that lets our teenagers carry on conversations with their friends while pretending to listen to their teachers, cable television that brings things into homes that we would never invite.

Just as I put away the Wii Fit and picked up a canoe paddle at the lake, may we all pause now and then to evaluate our technological choices, weigh the pros and cons of each, and eliminate or moderate as necessary. By emulating the peaceful, technology-free evenings in Amish homes, may we bring peace and quiet back to our own.

In Their Own Words

"I cannot imagine what it would be like if we had a telephone in the house. Even with the phone out in the barn, our teenager already calls her friends two or three times a week!"

16

TRANSPORTATION

The Amish do not drive or own cars for several reasons:

Humility: A lack of expensive, fancy cars provides less opportunity for pride.

Submission: Following the transportation rules demonstrates obedience to God, to the group, and to history.

Community: When travel is limited, everyone stays closer together and depends on each other.

Simplicity: Riding in a buggy provides a place for quiet and reflection, keeps life at a slower pace, and allows more time to look around and notice the beauty of the surroundings.

Thrift: Not owning a car eliminates loan payments, insurance, repairs, maintenance, and gasoline.

Family: Owning and driving one's own car provides too many opportunities for temptation and allows one to roam too far from home.

Separation: Their distinctive form of transportation provides a visible symbol of their separation from the world.

Other Forms of Transportation

Most districts permit the use of public transportation, though some have restrictions against air travel. Bicycles are used by some groups but not others. In Lancaster County, the simplest way to get around is on a scooter.

Many Amish communities also have "Amish taxis." These are cars with non-Amish drivers hired by the Amish to take them to work, appointments, and trips. In most cases, Amish taxis are not to be used to get to church.

Children on the farm enjoy riding in pony carts. These are like open-top buggies in miniature, pulled by ponies. Children learn to drive their pony carts at a very young age, and if their ponies are shod, they may even take them out on the road.

Buggy Variations and Types

Many outsiders are curious about the myriad of Amish rules regarding buggy ownership. These rules deal with color (black, gray, brown, white, or yellow), lights (battery powered or kerosene), style (covered or uncovered), mirrors, blinkers, safety markings, and more. Almost all aspects of buggies are regulated by the district in one way or another.

Different situations call for different types of buggies as well. The most common type is the family wagon, which has room for parents and children inside and has a window in the back.

Website Extras

Visit www.morefrommindy.com for photos and examples of various types of Amish buggies.

Takeaway Value

The Amish say that riding in a horse and buggy gives them a place for quiet and reflection, maintains the slow pace of their lives, and allows them more time to look around and notice the beauty of their surroundings. That probably doesn't hold true during a rainy rush hour on the main streets of Holmes or Lancaster Counties, but at other times and on less traveled roads, the slow pace of a buggy ride undoubtedly allows them to take in the sunshine, flowers, and rolling-hill vistas of farm after beautiful Amish farm.

We non-Amish probably won't be converting our garages into stables anytime soon, but we would do well to remember that our own forms of slower transportation, such as walking and biking, carry more benefits that merely providing good exercise. Leaving the car at home also allows us to slow the pace, pause and reflect, and enjoy nature, which is good for both the mind and the soul. Regardless of the mode of transportation we choose—foot or bike or scooter or golf cart or horse and buggy— the important thing is to take a cue from the Amish and travel without our cars whenever we can.

17

Occupations

Traditionally, the primary occupation of the Amish has been farming, for several reasons:

- In the early days of the Anabaptist movement, many fled into the countryside to avoid persecution. There they learned farming skills, which they later brought to America.

- The Amish believe that according to Scripture, farming is a sacred lifestyle and a way to connect closely with God.

- Farm work helps ingrain many Amish values, including a strong work ethic, patience, and simplicity.

The average Amish farm in Lancaster County has about 70 acres, and the crops commonly include corn, tobacco, alfalfa, and various grains. Unfortunately, rising land costs and decreased availability are prohibiting many younger Amish from continuing the farming tradition. Nowadays, the Amish work not only on farms but also in other trades, factories, restaurants, retail establishments, and so on. They are also starting up their own home-based businesses in record numbers—and frequently succeeding at it. Glenn Rifkin gives this report in the *New York Times*:

> The businesses, which favor such Amish skills as furniture-making, quilting, construction work and cooking, have been remarkably successful. Despite a lack of even a high school education… hundreds of Amish entrepreneurs have built profitable businesses based on the Amish values of high quality, integrity and hard work. A 2004 Goshen College study reported that the failure rate of Amish businesses is less than 5 percent, compared with a national small-business default rate that is far higher.

With the shift into entrepreneurship, of course, comes all sorts of challenges to the Amish way of life—new technologies, less time spent at home with family, and even mothers working outside of the home. How the Amish will face these challenges and continue to maintain an agrarian lifestyle remains to be seen.

In Their Own Words

"If we hang on to our beards, buggies, and bonnets

only so we can sell trinkets, we will indeed have sold our souls and our birthright for a bowl of porridge. Or to the other extreme, if we sacralize the name Amish to the point that we can hardly use it at all, we will have missed the point, which is that our lives are to be a light to the world and a service to Christ."

PART THREE:
PASSAGES

Lester let his eyes move over all of them, and without saying anything, he bowed his head. They followed. Leading out in a prayer he knew by memory, he prayed in High German and concluded, "Im Namen des Vater, des Sohns, und des Heiligen Geistes. Amen."

Not a head rose until Lester finished, and even then a brief hush hung over the room. Silence seemed to be in order.

None of the younger children understood the High German, but they knew it was used for spiritual occasions. It was God's language. The words carried a weight all their own. It was the sound used for important occasions— for church services, weddings, for Sunday morning songs, and for funerals. Whether the High German words were pronounced slowly by an elderly minister or rapidly by a younger speaker, it meant for them that the work of God was near.

—JERRY S. EICHER, *REBECCA'S PROMISE*

18

CHILDHOOD, FAMILY, AND OLD AGE

An Amish childhood is ideally filled with God, love, work, fun, and family—often all at the same time. Unlike modern Americans, the Amish do not strongly delineate between work time and playtime. Instead, they often combine the two, creating a hardworking and satisfying lifestyle. With such large families and close-knit communities, someone always seems to be available to share the load, the learning, and the laughter.

From a very early age, Amish children are taught that working hard is a vitally important virtue, and they are expected to learn how to plan and cook meals, guide a horse and buggy, plow the fields, and more. On Amish farms, young children may be given a small animal such as a chicken, duck, or goat that they alone must care for, which instills a strong work ethic and a sense of responsibility. They are also taught basic business principles, and older children may even derive a small income from their own produce stand or other home-based business. If children want something, they are encouraged to work for it, as the Amish believe that a gift given too easily too soon robs children of the joy of earning it for themselves.

The Amish take parenting very seriously, and when children are growing up, an enormous amount of time is invested in teaching them, guiding them by example, and working with them. As one Amish father says, "I could do this a lot faster by myself, but how else is he going to learn?" Boys and girls may work alongside their fathers in the fields or the workshop for hours each day. Girls are also often in the kitchen with their mothers, cooking or sewing or learning some other domestic skill.

Surprisingly, religious instruction and theological introspection are rare in the home. Instead, parents focus on quietly living out the principles of what they call *Demut* (the German word for humility) and expecting their children to do the same. By the time the kids reach school age, they are usually well-behaved, respectful, unpretentious, unentitled, and secure in their place in the family and the community.

An Amish childhood may not be as idyllic as it looks in pastel paintings and picture postcards, but in the best-case scenarios, it can come close. Amish or not, it's hard to imagine children who wouldn't enjoy caring for their very own animals and living in a tightly knit community, surrounded by parents and siblings who love them and willingly spend time with them.

Roles

Amish husbands and wives generally assume traditional male-female roles in the family. The husband is typically the breadwinner, and the wife cares for the home and the children. Mothers generally do not work outside of the home unless absolutely necessary.

The Elderly

When a couple's children are grown, they might pass down the farm to one of the younger generation and move themselves into the *Grossdaadi Haus,* a smaller house that is connected to or nearby the main house, much like an "in-law suite." There, the elder parents live out the rest of their lives, helping out with the younger ones when they can, providing wisdom and companionship to the family, and growing old with dignity and grace.

The Amish do not generally put their elderly in retirement homes.

The Flip Side

The good: Surrounded by family members and farm animals, Amish children often seem to have an endless supply of coworkers and playmates. By pitching in on the farm, children learn responsibility and develop a strong work ethic.

The bad: Farm work often puts Amish children in unsafe situations:

- Infants and toddlers may be tended by older siblings who are still too young and inexperienced themselves to be able to provide proper care.
- Children are sometimes in close proximity to dangerous farm equipment, often while barefoot.
- Boys as young as six or seven single-handedly manage huge teams of horses.

Erik Wesner, of the Amish America blog, reports seeing a little girl trundle around barefooted on the rusted, sharp-edged tin roof of a low structure adjacent to a barn. A good friend of mine still describes with horror the time she stopped to buy firewood from an Amish home, and as the father stood and chatted with them, he sent his three-year-old son to retrieve the ax!

Perhaps we non-Amish tend to carry our children's safety a little too far in the other direction, but the Amish attitude toward child safety can be disconcerting.

In Their Own Words

"If you live an honest and upright life there is no need to 'talk the talk.' Your life speaks for itself."

19

SCHOOL

Approximately 10 percent of all Amish children go to public schools. The remaining 90 percent attend private parochial schools that are run by their communities. Amish schools are directed by small boards of Amish fathers who approve the curriculum, hire the teachers, maintain the buildings, and oversee the budgets. The buildings themselves are usually one- or two-room schoolhouses.

Amish schoolhouses are usually large enough to accommodate 25 to 30 children of various grade levels, with separate boys' and girls' outhouse-style bathrooms outside.

Each school has one teacher, usually an unmarried Amish woman in her late teens or early twenties who has been chosen because of her Christian character, Amish values, and teaching ability. Two-room schoolhouses or single-room schoolhouses with more than 30 children may have a second teacher or a teacher's assistant. Older students often help with the younger students. In schools for Amish children with special needs, the teacher-student ratio is about one to four.

Like their non-Amish counterparts, Amish children enter first grade around age 6. School hours and term lengths are similar to those in public school, though the Amish generally don't take as much time off for holidays. In Lancaster County, for example, Christmas is only a two-day break, so the school year ends in early May.

Amish children conclude their education with the eighth grade. They usually walk to school, but where distance is an issue, school buses are hired.

The Amish call their students *scholars*.

Amish Schools and the Law

Prior to the late 1930s, the Amish usually attended small, rural public schools in or near their communities. From 1937 to 1954, as public school boards began consolidating these into larger schools, the Amish became concerned that their children were being taught too far from home by teachers the family didn't know, they were getting an education that neither complemented nor facilitated an agricultural lifestyle, and they were being exposed to too much of the outside world. Afraid that their communities were being undermined, some Amish responded by building their own private schools, hiring their own teachers, and limiting education to the eighth grade.

This did not always sit well with the authorities. School officials considered the Amish teachers uncertified and undereducated, and the lack of high school–level instruction unacceptable. A period of unrest and controversy followed, and some Amish fathers were arrested, fined, and even jailed for taking a stand. Some compromises were reached, but the issue finally came to a head in 1972, when the case of *Wisconsin v. Yoder* reached the U.S. Supreme Court. Finding in favor of the Amish, the court determined once and for all that Amish schools were to be allowed and that forcing Amish children to attend any school past the eighth grade was a violation of their religious freedom.

Curriculum

Though the curriculum varies from district to district, most Amish students study arithmetic, spelling, reading, grammar, history, geography, social studies, German, and penmanship. Except for "nature studies," science is generally not included in the curriculum. (Amish farmers deal frequently with the science of agriculture, but science as a school subject is considered suspect.) Religion is not taught, though Amish values are woven throughout their textbooks. Some religious rituals are included in the school day, such as the reading of an opening prayer. Classes are usually not given in computers, music, art, drama, or physical education.

Classes are taught in English, and the children are expected to speak English both in the classroom and on the playground. (Most first graders start school with only a rudimentary knowledge of English, so they are usually given some leeway until they become fluent.)

Amish adults who require further learning on a particular topic, such as bookkeeping, will teach themselves, learn from a coworker, or take a correspondence course. In some communities, when a high school diploma is required for a job, Amish youth may be allowed to get a GED.

Think About It

Amish schools do not normally emphasize critical analysis, independent thinking, creativity, or individuality. Instead, they focus on the Amish values of obedience, respect, kindness, cooperation, and submission. Their limited education may not prepare them to function in a high-tech world, but they feel that it does sufficiently prepare them for low-tech Amish life and work.

Takeaway Value

The National PTA has published a list of the "Top 10 Things Teachers Wish Parents Would Do." Not surprisingly, the Amish have already been doing many of these things for years, such as setting a good example and encouraging students to do their best. Number ten, however, is central to the way Amish parents operate: "Accept your responsibility as parents. Don't expect the school and teachers to take over your obligations...Teach children self-discipline and respect for others at home—don't rely on teachers and schools to teach these basic behaviors and attitudes."

The Amish would never dream of leaving parental matters such as those described above in the hands of teachers. Instead, they know they are the primary authority figures in their children's lives and are responsible to raise them up in the way that they should go. We would do well to follow their example in this matter—for the sake of our children, their classmates, and their teachers.

20

RUMSPRINGA

Despite the common use of the term—even in this book—there's actually no such thing as an "Amish child." The more correct wording would be "child of Amish parents" or "child in an Amish community." That's because people aren't *born* Amish; they must *become* Amish, which is a voluntary process that happens at the cusp of adulthood, usually in the late teens or early twenties. That's when those who have been raised in Amish homes decide whether they are going to accept the Amish faith and be baptized into its membership.

Before that, however, every Amish teen experiences *Rumspringa*, which is Pennsylvania Dutch for "running around." The goal of *Rumspringa* is to relax the rules a bit, to allow teenagers to experience a taste of the outside world, to find a mate (they hope), and to give them enough freedom to make an informed, independent, and mature decision about whether they want to become Amish like their parents or instead leave the

Amish faith and forge a new life on their own. Those who choose not to join the church are not shunned.

Rumspringa usually begins at age 16 and lasts for several years. During this time period, though teens still live at home and have all of the same obligations and responsibilities as before, the rules of the *Ordnung* are relaxed. Parents and church leaders "look the other way" as teens are allowed to experiment with their newfound freedom. Teens get their own private bedroom and sometimes even slip away at night to meet up with friends or dates.

In a conservative district, *Rumspringa* might include flirting at a group singing or riding home from church with someone of the opposite sex in a courting wagon. In a more liberal district, *Rumspringa* can mean obtaining a driver's license, buying a car, using electronics, buying a cell phone, and more. In worst-case scenarios, teens may get involved with sex, drugs, alcohol, smoking, or spending their weekends at wild *Rumspringa* parties, notorious beer bashes that include both Amish and non-Amish teenagers and young adults.

Eventually, young adults in Amish communities must choose between turning their backs on the world and accepting the faith of their parents, or making somewhat of a break from their homes and family and fully embracing the outside world. All teens know that if they decide to go with the church, they are making a lifelong commitment. As a part of the baptism process, they will take vows that commit them to the community, the church leadership, and the *Ordnung* until the day they die.

Surprisingly, in the end, 85 percent of teens raised in Amish homes choose to join the church.

Fascinating Fact

In some conservative districts, teens on *Rumspringa* may be allowed to enjoy an old Amish custom known as *Uneheliche beischlaf*, the practice of "bundling" or "bed courtship." Bundling allows an unmarried male and female to spend the night together in the same bed, ostensibly without having sex. They may each be wrapped in their own blanket, or she may wear a special preventative gown. The couple is left alone in the female's bedroom, and the parents go on to bed. The young man is allowed to spend most of the night but is expected to leave the home before morning milking time, which is usually around four or four thirty.

According to author Richard Stevick, this practice was brought to America by European immigrants in the eighteenth century and was far more prevalent in the past than it is today. He estimates that fewer than 10 percent of Amish districts still allow bundling. Most Amish seem reticent to discuss the custom at all.

Proponents of the practice assert that it teaches self-discipline while allowing the couple to get to know each other in a warm and comfortable setting. Premarital sex is not allowed, though most critics of the practice insist that it often becomes inevitable. In the event that a premarital pregnancy results, most Amish teens will quickly join the church and then get married.

21

BAPTISM

The only formal religious instruction classes that most Amish ever attend are those that prepare them for baptism. These classes are held on Sunday mornings during the first 30 or 40 minutes of the worship service and are taught by the bishop and the ministers in a room separate from the rest of the congregation.

When a young person decides he wants to be baptized, he presents himself for the first of eight or nine classes taught over the course of several months. Baptisms occur only once a year, so many parents of teens hold their breath, waiting to see if their children are among those who choose to attend the class. (If not, their children will have another year of *Rumspringa* before their next opportunity to do so.) Many Amish consider themselves successful parents only if their children join the church.

The baptism preparation classes primarily focus on the Dordrecht Confession of Faith, a document written in 1632 that espouses the key beliefs of Anabaptism.

Candidates learn in depth about each of the 18 articles and in many cases will also be taught the specifics of their own local *Ordnung*. During the months that candidates are attending these every-other-Sunday classes, they are expected to eliminate all trappings of *Rumspringa* from their lives, which means selling their cars, getting rid of their English clothes, giving up technological devices, growing out their hair, and so on. In some districts, they must quit attending weekend parties by the third session in order to move into full compliance with the *Ordnung*.

Repeatedly throughout the preparation process, the young people are asked if they are certain they want to be baptized and join the church. In fact, each session begins with the youth stating, "I am a seeker desiring to be part of this church of God." The Amish strongly emphasize informed, voluntary adult baptism. Those candidates who are hesitant, rebellious, or too questioning may decide that they weren't ready after all and drop out of the classes until the next year. Those who make it to the end have one final session (which includes their parents), the day before baptism Sunday, where once again they are asked if they are certain they want to proceed. At this point, the male candidates are also asked if they are willing to serve in the ministry if they are ever chosen by lot.

Baptism is usually held on the same Sunday as the

fall Communion service. Candidates take vows and then kneel in front of the bishop, who confirms their vows and baptizes them one by one. Amish baptism is done by the bishop placing his cupped hands on each head as the deacon pours water into those hands from a pitcher. After all are baptized, the bishop welcomes each male in turn with a holy kiss while his wife does the same to the females.

Once baptized, members are bound to the Amish faith for the rest of their lives.

22

COURTSHIP AND MARRIAGE

Courtship among the Amish is done with much discretion, and engagements are not usually made public until one to six weeks prior to the wedding. A bride and groom's closest friends and family members may be told, but otherwise only the church leaders are informed and not the congregation at large.

For an engagement to be made official, the groom must go to his bishop, declare his intentions, and acquire a *Zeugnis*, which is a letter of good standing from his church. If the bishop is aware of any sinful behavior or need for correction, he deals with it at that time.

Once the groom acquires the *Zeugnis*, he delivers it to the bride's minister or deacon. That church leader will visit the bride, confirm that she desires to marry the groom, and discuss any sin or other concerns in her life. After this meeting, if all is satisfactory, the leader will wait until the appropriate time and then "publish" or announce the engagement to the church.

In some settlements, weddings are limited to certain times of the year and even specific days of the week.

Lancaster County weddings, for example, are held on Tuesdays and Thursdays in October, November, or December. Weddings in Geuaga County, Ohio, are held in the summer.

Amish weddings can be quite large, often with 300 to 500 guests. The Amish don't use caterers, so the food preparation alone can be a tremendous undertaking. Fortunately, plenty of volunteers are always available to help out, and the communities have been through so many weddings before that everyone is familiar with the various duties required.

Weddings are usually held in the bride's parents' home, barn, or shop. The regular Sunday benches are used, though if the wedding is large, benches from several other nearby communities may be needed as well. In a carefully orchestrated event, family and friends work to prepare the wedding feast and ready the home for the celebration.

Ceremony

An Amish wedding ceremony is similar in many ways to their regular Sunday worship service. As the congregation sings the opening hymns, the couple is brought into a separate room with the bishop and ministers for a time of "admonition and encouragement" called the *Abroth*. This lasts about 20 or 30 minutes, and then all rejoin the congregation for the rest of the service. As on Sundays, an opening sermon, a prayer, a Bible reading, and a main sermon are included. The bride and groom each have two attendants. In most districts, the couple wears brand-new versions of their usual Sunday attire, with one exception: The groom sports his first "real" Amish hat, one with a broader brim to indicate that he is married.

During the main sermon, the bishop asks the couple a series of questions, the affirmation of which will serve as their vows. This is followed by the reading of a prayer and the pronouncing of the couple as man and wife. The bride and groom do not kiss but instead return to their seats for the rest of the sermon. Additional sermons and commentary are given by other church leaders, followed by final prayers and songs. The entire event is very solemn and lasts about three hours. When it is over, the bride will switch from the black head covering of a single girl to the white *Kapp* of a married woman.

The post-wedding celebration varies from district to district, but it focuses on the newly married couple and on the feast.

Website Extras

Visit www.morefrommindy.com for more information about Amish wedding celebrations.

The New Couple

The new husband and wife usually spend their wedding night at the home of her parents. The very next morning, they are expected to rise at four or five to help with the massive cleanup effort. Other close friends or relatives may join in to help as well.

It is not unusual for the bride and groom to continue living in her parents' home for several weeks or months following the wedding. On the weekends, the couple is kept busy paying visits to the homes of the numerous relatives and friends who came to their wedding. In each home, they will be greeted warmly, share a meal, enjoy conversation, and in many cases be given their wedding presents.

When the visits have all been made, the couple might move into a small house near the groom's parents' home. There, they will set up housekeeping and finally begin their life together in their own home as husband and wife.

Fascinating Fact

In some regions, despite all of the secrecy regarding courtships, nosy community members can usually figure out which families will be having a fall wedding by the amount of celery they've planted in their garden that year. Celery is a late-growing vegetable, so it's a common fixture at weddings both as a main food and in table decorations. If the guest list will be large, as it usually is, the celery must be grown in great quantities, far more than a family would otherwise need.

23

DEATH

Most Amish folks accept death gracefully. They consider it the ultimate submission to God, the surrender of the living body to the grave. Amish or not, dealing with death is never easy, but being surrounded by an ever-present group of believers in times of grief can be a great comfort and aid.

Funeral planning for the Amish is generally simpler than for the non-Amish. Tradition dictates everything from casket style to burial clothing to the post-funeral meal, so few decisions have to be made.

When an Amish person dies, news spreads throughout the community primarily by word of mouth. In response, Amish friends and neighbors spring into action, helping with funeral arrangements, farm and household chores, and the preparation of the home for the funeral. The extended family of the bereaved usually contacts more distant relatives and friends to give them the news.

The Amish prefer to die at home whenever possible.

Whether death comes there or in a hospital, the body of the deceased is handled in the same manner: A non-Amish mortician retrieves it, embalms it, and brings it to the home. There, family members of the same sex dress the embalmed body in burial clothes and place the deceased in a simple wooden casket. The casket goes on display in a main room of the first floor, usually the living room, where it will remain until the funeral. Visitation by friends and family takes place there. Volunteers continue to take care of all funeral preparations, housework, and farm work. This leaves the family free to focus on the relatives and friends who come to pay their respects.

The grave is dug by hand by family or friends in an Amish cemetery. The funeral is usually held on the third day after the death, unless that happens to fall on a Sunday. Amish funerals are about an hour and a half long and consist of various ministers giving sermons and reading hymns, Scriptures, and prayers. There are no songs, eulogies, or flowers.  After the funeral, everyone proceeds to the cemetery for a brief word graveside. The casket, which typically has no handles, is lowered into the ground with ropes and then covered with dirt.

In a final display of humility, Amish headstones are almost always of equal size and contain no extra information or fancy embellishments.

After the ceremony, close family and friends return to the home where they share a meal that has been prepared by the community.

Fascinating Fact

Most Amish women are buried wearing the same white Kapp and apron they wore on their wedding day.

PART FOUR:
OUTSIDE WORLD

There was no denying that by allowing an outsider to stay in her house, Rachel was flirting with disobedience to the rules by which she and her people lived…She was in very real danger of facing the consequences that could come from breaking her vows to God and the church—vows that were meant to be valid for a lifetime.

Resentment suddenly gave way to a chilling sense of dread. She knew herself to be Amish in every way. She was thoroughly and uncompromisingly Plain. To go against the Ordnung would mean not only to go against everything she believed, but it could even put her at risk of the terrible Meidung—the shunning.

The very word stirred fear in her. She would rather die than be cut off, expelled from her family, her friends, from the only way of life she had ever known.

—BJ HOFF, *RACHEL'S SECRET*

24

TOURISM AND MEDIA

I n the book *The Amish and the Media*, authors Diane Zimmerman Umble and David Weaver-Zercher address our collective obsession with all things Amish.

> The Amish are fascinating, at least to those of us who operate from different assumptions about dress, travel, education, technology, and success— or to put it more sociologically, different assumptions about individuation, specialization, and differentiation. Religiously informed decisions that the Amish have made over the past 150 years have produced not only a visibly distinct culture but also a viscerally fascinating one.

That fascination, according to Umble and Weaver-Zercher, "is not an inevitable, let alone accidental, result of differences between the Amish and the English. Rather, this fascination has been created and sustained to a large degree by the media."

No doubt, our ideas of the Amish people, what

they believe, and how they live are greatly influenced by the tourism, film, television, publishing, and news industries.

Tourism

Tourists often come to Amish settlements to participate in what Umble and Weaver-Zercher call "the myth of the pastoral." This myth implies that Amish life is wholesome and old-fashioned, simple and perfect and good. Dining on a bounty of farm-fresh delights every day, the Amish have no cares or problems, are free from all technology, and are in fact uniquely pure and special. No wonder we come to gawk!

The myth carries some truth, but the fact remains that the Amish are human beings with normal human problems, conflicts, and frustrations. Their history has its unattractive parts, as does their society. Much about the Amish people is good, but they are not, in fact, perfect. They are simply people.

The Amish-based tourism industry, however, tends to ignore this fact and focus heavily on the more visible parts of their culture: their charming manner of dress and speech, their patchwork farms, their homemade food, and their beautiful quilts and furniture. The word *Amish* draws tourists and customers, which results in the good, the bad, and the ugly. In Amish country, for every helpful information center there's a neon-signed tourist trap; for every tasteful furniture store offering Amish-made goods, there's a cartoon rendering of a bearded men in a black hat advertising "authentic" Amish fast food.

The exploitation isn't always intentional. Several years ago, for example, I attended a fictional multimedia presentation about a boy on Rumspringa who was trying to decide whether or not to be baptized into the Amish church. The production was slick and professional, but when it was over I realized that the story had never once mentioned God or Jesus or faith, instead focusing only on whether the teen could bear to give up driving his beloved sports car. Somehow, I couldn't help feeling that the producers had missed the point!

Then there are the more blatant attempts to milk the Amish cash cow: "Amish goods" that were actually made in China, "Amish buggy rides" given by non-Amish wearing costumes, tacky tourist shops overflowing with horse-and-buggy pencil sharpeners and other "Amish" souvenirs that an Amish person would have no use for whatsoever.

Misinformation and exploitation abound, but the sadder truth is that the places that are knowledgeable and respectful of the Amish draw fewer tourists than those that are flashy and sensationalistic and oftentimes downright misleading.

Feature Films

Many popular feature films have focused on Amish life, but none has done more to spread the Amish myth than the Peter Weir film *Witness*, featuring Harrison Ford and Kelly McGillis. This film has been criticised by many Amish as being inconsistent with their lifestyle and culture.

This shouldn't be too surprising. The purpose of a romantic drama, after all, is to entertain, not to inform. Filmmakers have always taken liberties with the truth in order to create more exciting stories. Unfortunately, a person whose entire knowledge of the Amish comes from feature films like *Witness*—not to mention *For Richer or Poorer, Kingpin*, and others—is at best underinformed and at worst sorely misinformed.

Documentaries

Documentarians have a larger responsibility to stick with the facts than those who are making fictional films, so we should be able to safely assume that documentaries about the Amish come closer to revealing the true picture of Amish life. The problem is that documentaries still must be entertaining and consumer friendly, however, which means that they often fall at two ends of the spectrum, what Umble and Weaver-Zercher call either "sympathetic, myth-enhancing pastorals like *A People of Preservation* or myth-busting and highly entertaining but narrowly focused and nonrepresentative sensationalism like *Devil's Playground*."

Neither of these two films plays fast and loose with the facts, but both provide specific angles on certain facets of Amish life. This, in turn, causes many people to apply those small truths to the Amish as a whole, which is a mistake.

Reality Television

If the feature films and the documentaries aren't getting it right, how about reality TV? In July 2004, the reality show *Amish in the City* debuted, featuring five Amish youth on *Rumspringa* in a modern home where they lived for a time among five non-Amish youth. By filming the inevitable culture clash, the producers hoped to highlight the similarities and differences between two such disparate worlds.

In the end, the series was criticized as exploitative and offensive. It also didn't do much to advance the cause of truth about Amish life.

News Media

The news media cannot always be counted on for accuracy or balance when it comes to the Amish either. News reports still need a hook, after all, and the hooks that come from an Amish drug bust or a travesty of violence have less to do with the incidents themselves than with our image of who the Amish are and how the incidents relate to that. One need look no further than the media coverage of the Nickel Mines school shooting to see how shockingly fast the big story turned from the violence perpetrated on a group of school children to the "larger issues" of Amish forgiveness.

I would contend that the news media did both the Amish and the non-Amish a great disservice by focusing their reports on the forgiveness angle rather than on larger, more important issues, such as school violence, child safety, and mental illness.

Other Sources

Where is the good news in all of this? Despite the problems with tourism, feature films, documentaries, television, and news media, in my opinion at least three places are providing helpful information.

Academia. Thanks to esteemed authors and scholars such as Kraybill, Weaver-Zercher, Hostetler, Stevick, and Nolt, numerous resources are available for those who want to get an accurate, balanced view of the Amish.

Website Extras

Visit www.morefrommindy.com for a list of works by these accomplished authors.

Fiction. Certainly, Amish fiction authors bring to any story their own slant and agenda, especially with regard to the salvation element of the Amish experience. Still, most authors of Amish fiction seem to be taking pains to get their facts correct and present them in a balanced manner. By setting fictional tales in realistic worlds, Amish fiction authors are inviting readers to a fuller understanding of Amish life in all its shades of black, white, and gray.

Historical societies and information centers. Many historical organizations offer accurate and interesting information about the Amish and other Anabaptist groups. In some regions, these places offer helpful volunteers, printed resources, and even tour guide services. Should you choose to visit a region of Amish tourism, you would do well to begin your visit not with the flashiest simulated Amish experience but with the local historical society or tourist information center.

By drawing our information from these sources, may we leave the fallacies and agendas behind and instead focus on the fascinating, complex, and *true* world of the Amish.

25

MYTHS VERSUS FACTS

Myth: The Amish are a cult.

Fact: The Amish are Christians and do not fit the modern, generally accepted criteria for what constitutes a cult. They may be confused as one because they follow a very restrictive set of rules and face excommunication (shunning) for certain infractions of those rules. However, unlike a cult, the Amish religion is not centered on a single human authority, they do not require their members to pool their finances, and the tenets of their faith are compatible with most major Protestant denominations. Thus, they are not a cult but simply an ultraconservative Christian faith culture.

Myth: The Amish think they are the only ones who are going to heaven.

Fact: Despite their strong faith and regulated lifestyle, most Amish do not claim an assurance of heaven even for themselves, much less for anyone else. Instead, they live in the Christian hope that they will go to heaven but believe it would be prideful or presumptuous to know for sure. In the same vein, the Amish are surprisingly nonjudgmental about other religions. They follow the teachings of the Sermon on the Mount, which includes the admonition, "Do not judge, or you too will be judged." They may pray for themselves and others, but they leave the prospect of heaven up to God alone.

Myth: The Amish don't pay taxes.

Fact: The Amish pay the same taxes as the non-Amish, with one exception: Amish who are self-employed may be exempted from paying Social Security tax. (In fact, any American has the right to waive Social Security coverage for religious reasons.) They believe that care for the elderly and unemployed should come from within the faith community and not from the government; because of this, they almost never collect Social Security benefits or Medicare.

Myth: The Amish don't go to doctors or hospitals.

Fact: Most Amish have no restrictions against seeking modern medical care. For financial or holistic reasons, they may be less likely to seek out professional help for lesser ailments or injuries, but when the situation warrants the care of a physician or hospital, they will go. Because the Amish do not have medical insurance, excessive medical bills are usually paid for by the Amish community.

Myth: The Amish don't use banks, but instead stash their cash in their homes and pockets.

Fact: The Amish use bank accounts, not piggy banks, to store their money. In fact, a common sight in Lancaster County is a horse and buggy waiting in line at the local bank's drive-through window!

Myth: The Amish aren't allowed to vote.

Fact: Most Amish are allowed to vote, though voter turnout is usually low. They do not run for public office.

Myth: The Amish reject all modern technology.

Fact: The Amish are very selective about the devices and innovations that members are allowed to possess, but they do not reject all modern technology outright. When a new technology becomes available within a district, church leaders will evaluate its potential for causing harm to Amish life and values and then make a decision accordingly. No technology, regardless of how labor-saving it may be, is permissible if the leaders determine that it will be spiritually detrimental to the community.

Myth: The Amish have arranged marriages.

Fact: The Amish freely choose their own spouses. This myth probably arose from the church approval process to which all engagements are subject. When a couple wants to marry, they must both be members in good standing of the Amish church and provide proof of such when necessary to the bride's church leaders. If the match is satisfactory, the engagement is "published" (announced to the congregation) by the bishop.

Myth: Amish fathers paint their gates blue to advertise the presence of marriageable daughters.

Fact: This is purely a myth and has no basis in reality.

Myth: Amish women are required to give birth at home.

Fact: Though many Amish women prefer to have their children at home with the aid of a midwife, others opt for a hospital or birthing center instead. Most Amish couples are free to choose whatever environment works best for them.

Myth: The Amish work hard so they can earn their way into heaven.

Fact: The Amish believe that salvation comes through grace by faith. The reason they work so hard has to do with the way they have chosen to live out their Christian walk in their day-to-day lives.

Myth: Because they believe in nonresistance, the Amish do not own or handle guns.

Fact: The Amish have no problem with guns as long as they are not used against people. Many Amish are avid hunters who use both guns and compound bows.

Myth: The Amish are not allowed to use birth control.

Fact: Many districts discourage or outright forbid the use of any form of birth control. In some districts, however, family planning is a private matter left to the discretion of husband and wife. The Amish encourage having large families, so family planning is not usually necessary. It is, however, sometimes permissible.

Myth: The Amish don't use any power sources.

Fact: Amish homes are not wired for public utilities, but they do use many other sources of power, including propane, kerosene, batteries, wind, water, and the sun.

Myth: The Amish never go to restaurants or shopping centers.

Fact: The Amish do go to restaurants and shopping centers. Because frugality is a key value for the Amish, very few families eat out on a weekly basis, but there are usually no restrictions on going to restaurants or shopping centers when the budget allows.

Myth: The Amish are inbred.

Fact: The term *inbreeding* commonly refers to procreation by close relatives, usually siblings or first cousins. In that sense, the Amish are not inbred, as most districts forbid marriages between anything less than second cousins. Unfortunately, the Amish do suffer from what is known as the "founder effect," which can have its own negative genetic results. Most Amish can trace their genetic roots back to a small set of common ancestors. Through many generations of genetic intermixing, mutations of their DNA have caused the proliferation of rare disorders—for example, dwarfism and maple-syrup-urine disease—that tend to be much more common among the Amish than in the wider population. They also have a greater incidence of rare blood types.

The flip side of this problematic situation is that DNA researchers have been able to study the Amish to glean information from their genes, information that can help to identify and treat a host of rare and common genetically influenced disorders (such as diabetes) that affect both the Amish and the population at large. For the most part, the Amish have been extremely cooperative with researchers, allowing blood draws for scientific study. In turn, researchers at places like the Clinic for Special Children in Lancaster County work closely with the Amish to help treat and prevent the rare disorders that occur with such a high frequency among them.

Myth: All Amish are Christians.

Myth: No Amish are Christians.

Fact: The Amish faith is based on Christian tenets, so in theory, anyone who genuinely accepts those tenets is in fact a Christian. As in any religion, however, some people pay lip service to their denomination's beliefs without ever internalizing its true messages. In that sense, people of the Amish faith are no different from other Protestants and Catholics around the world. Some people choose a particular faith because of tradition, or because they want to be a part of the community, or because they've never known any other way of life. But some make the choice they do because they love the Lord, believe on his Son, and want to follow him regardless of the cost. As to which individuals of *any* Christian faith are genuinely Christians, that lies between them and God and can't be known for sure by anyone else, at least not on this side of heaven.

Myth: The Amish are all good.

Myth: The Amish are all bad.

Fact: The Amish are normal, regular, human people.

Their way of life is different from many others', but that doesn't change the fact that there are good Amish and bad Amish and a whole lot in between—just like the rest of the world.

Website Extras

Has *A Pocket Guide to Amish Life* been helpful to you? Would you like to learn even more about the Amish? Then don't miss www.morefrommindy .com, where you'll find…

- more Fascinating Facts and Takeaway Values

- expanded information relating to many of the chapters in this book

- photos and examples about a variety of Amish-related topics in this book

- biblical support for Amish practices

- common Amish idioms

- a thorough glossary of Amish-related words and phrases

- a list of helpful resources for further study, including contact information and website links

- a complete bibliography for this pocket guide

26

WHY ARE THEY AMISH?

In the course of writing this book, I have thought a lot about Amish life, about the good and the bad, the pros and the cons.

Picturing myself in their world, I first think about the cons. I imagine all their rules and how I would chafe so strongly against them. I think of not being allowed to have electricity or choose my own style of clothing or pursue my education. I think of how I would resent being discouraged from having theological discussions or prohibited from singing along with a praise band in church. I look at my children and can't fathom limiting their education or their occupational choices. As charming as the Amish life can seem from the outside looking in, there are many reasons I would never want to be Amish.

And yet...

And yet there is much to be said for the Amish way of life, much to admire, much to emulate. Their peaceful existence. Their strong work ethic. The way they constantly strive for Christlikeness. It draws me in a way that I don't quite understand. Still, I know that living in their world couldn't work for me.

What I've been trying to understand is why it works for *them*.

Truly, why are they Amish? As I researched this book, I came up with several answers to that question.

First, I believe that the Amish find tremendous personal satisfaction in belonging to something bigger than themselves. Their incredibly strong family and community ties make the difficult parts of life easier, the rules worth following, the lifestyle worth living. Belonging to a group of believers with whom one worships, fellowships, goes to school, works, and plays would be incredibly fulfilling. Imagine knowing that if your barn burned down, your friends would show up and build you another one. Imagine facing catastrophic medical issues with the knowledge that your community would shoulder the financial burden beyond what you were able to pay. Imagine living in a community that was a real community, where everyone's duty was to love each other, care for each other, befriend each other, and even discipline each other—all because God requires them to. Imagine the safety net that would provide! In a world where we hardly know our next-door neighbors, the thought of being that strongly connected to an entire people group is appealing indeed.

Second, the family structure provides much to admire as well. Amish children spend an enormous amount of time in the company of their parents. The Amish see childrearing as their most important job, and they are always instructing, loving, guiding, teaching. Who wouldn't enjoy knowing that their highest calling was simply to be God in the flesh to one's own children?

Third, the Amish have a wonderful way to grow old. They have no nursing homes, no institutions to care for the elderly. Instead, families stay together, with the older parents shifting into the *Grossdaadi Haus*, where they can age with grace and dignity. They often end their days right there at home.

Fourth is their calm and simple day-to-day life. Without televisions, things are quieter and more peaceful; without telephones and computers, life has far fewer interruptions. Given the Amish emphasis on simplicity and serenity, one can easily imagine lingering after dinner with the family, reading or sewing, sharing news of the day, the children quietly playing nearby.

Finally, I believe that the Amish enjoy living as they do because God is so very central to all of it. The Amish strive mightily to live within his will, follow the Scriptures, and truly be in the world but not of the world. For those who embrace Christ as Savior, theirs is a joyous and noble path indeed.

That's why it works for them.

Perhaps this is also why Amish fiction is so popular: Though we can't imagine life without modern conveniences and unlimited entertainment options, something is incredibly appealing to us about living fully for God in a home that is technology free, family focused, and surrounded by a loving and supportive community. Through reading, we can experience all of that vicariously as we briefly visit their world.

But then, as we put away the books and come back out again, let us bring with us all that is fine and good and true about the Amish.

Then may we apply it to our non-Amish lives.

Website Extras

Turn the page to find a handy topical index to this Pocket Guide. For an expanded, more detailed index, visit www.morefrommindy.com.

TOPICAL INDEX

Topical Index

About the Author

A Pocket Guide to Amish Life is Mindy's thirteenth book with Harvest House Publishers and her second foray into the world of the Amish, which began in 2009 with the release of her bestselling Amish mystery, *Shadows of Lancaster County*. Other books by Mindy include the nonfiction *The House That Cleans Itself* as well as the stand-alone mystery novels *Under the Cajun Moon* and *Whispers of the Bayou*, the Smart Chick Mystery series, and the Million Dollar Mysteries series.

Mindy is a popular speaker and playwright as well as a former singer and stand-up comedian. She lives near Valley Forge, Pennsylvania, with her husband and two daughters.

Visit Mindy's website at
www.mindystarnsclark.com.

About the Artist

Amy Hanson Starns has worked as a graphic artist for more than 25 years, designing logos, album covers, magazine editorials, advertisements, and more. She enjoys teaching and sharing art with children and young adults. She has two grown children and lives in Flagstaff, Arizona. Amy earned her degree in Fine Arts from California State University.